Arizona Bingo Book

COMPLETE BINGO GAME IN A BOOK

Written By Rebecca Stark
Educational Books 'n' Bingo

TITLE: Arizona Bingo
AUTHOR: Rebecca Stark

ISBN 978-0-87386-496-1

Educational Books 'n' Bingo

Printed in the U.S.A.

DIRECTIONS

INCLUDED:

List of Terms

Templates for Additional Terms and Clues

2 Clues per Term

30 Unique Bingo Sheets (To cut out or copy)

Sheet of Markers (to copy and distribute)

1. **Either cut apart the book or make copies of ALL the sheets. You might want to make an extra copy of the clue sheets to use for introduction and review. Keep the sheets in an envelope for easy reuse.**

2. Cut apart the call sheets with terms and clues.

3. Pass out one bingo sheet per student. There are enough unique sheets for a class of 30.

4. Pass out the markers. You may cut apart the markers included in this book or use any other small items of your choice. Students can also mark the sheets themselves; recopy the sheets as needed for additional games.

5. Decide whether or not you will require the entire sheet to be filled. Requiring the entire sheet to be filled provides a better review. However, if you have a short time to fill, you may prefer to have them do the just the border or some other format. Tell the class before you begin what is required.

6. There are 50 terms. Read the list before you begin. If there are any terms that have not been covered in class, you may want to read to the students the term and clues before you begin.

7. There is a blank space in the middle of each sheet. You can instruct the students to use it as a free space or you can write in answers to cover terms not included. Of course, in this case you would create your own clues. (Templates provided.)

8. Shuffle the sheets and place them in a pile. Two or three clues are provided for each term. If you plan to play the game with the same group more than once, you might want to choose a different clue for each game. If not, you may choose to use more than one clue.

9. Be sure to keep the sheets you have used for the present game in a separate pile. When a student calls, "Bingo," he or she will have to verify that the correct answers are on his or her sheet AND that the markers were placed in response to the proper questions. Pull out the sheets that are on the student's sheet keeping them in the order they were used in the game. Read each clue as it was given and ask the student to identify the correct answer from his or her sheet.

10. If the student has the correct answers on the sheet AND has shown that they were marked in response to the *correct questions,* then that student is the winner and the game is over. If the student does not have the correct answers on the sheet OR he or she marked the answers in response to *the wrong questions,* then the game continues until there is a proper winner.

11. If you want to play again, reshuffle the sheets and begin again.

Have fun

TERMS INCLUDED

Anthem	Judicial Branch
Apache(s)	Lake Havasu
Arizona Territory	Lake Mead
Basin and Ridge	Legislative Branch
Bolo Tie(s)	Livestock
Border	Manufacture
Buttes	Monument Valley
Cactus Wren	Motto
César E. Chávez	Navajo
Climate (-ic)	Palo Verde
Cochise	Petrified Wood
Colorado Plateau	Phoenix
Copper	Pueblos
Counties	Ridge-nosed Rattlesnake
Crop(s)	Ringtail
Francisco Vasquez de Coronado	River(s)
Executive Branch	Saguaro Cactus
Flag	Seal
Flagstaff	Sedona
Gadsden Purchase	Tohono O'odham
Geronimo	Transition Zone
Grand Canyon	Tree Frog
Hoover Dam	Turquoise
Hopi	Tucson
Humphreys Peak	Union

Additional Terms

Choose as many additional terms as you would like and write them in the squares.
Repeat each as desired.
Cut out the squares and randomly distribute them to the class.
Instruct the students to place their square on the center space of their card.

Arizona Bingo

Clues for Additional Terms

Write three clues for each of your additional terms.

<table>
<tr><td>

_____

1.

2.

3.

</td><td>

_____

1.

2.

3.

</td></tr>
<tr><td>

_____

1.

2.

3.

</td><td>

_____

1.

2.

3.

</td></tr>
<tr><td>

_____

1.

2.

3.

</td><td>

_____

1.

2.

3.

</td></tr>
</table>

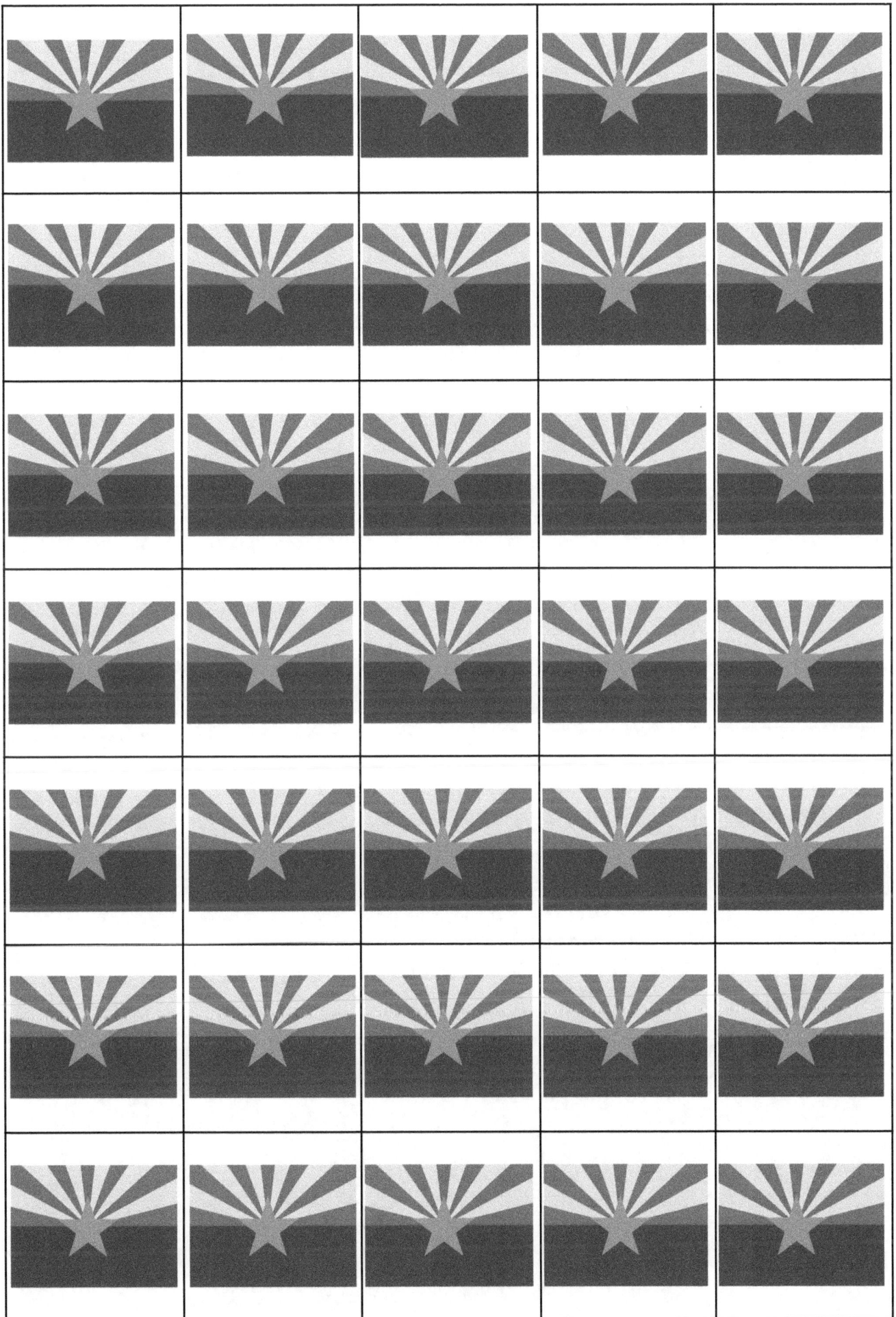

Anthem
1. "Arizona March Song," was written in 1915 by Margaret Rowe Clifford. It was officially designated the Arizona state ___ in 1919.
2. The song "Arizona," written by country-music singer Rex Allen Jr., was designated an alternate state ___ in 1982.

Apache(s)
1. The seat of tribal government for the White Mountain ___ Reservation is Whiteriver.
2. ___ nations include the Western ___, the Chiricahua, the Mescalero, the Jicarrilla, the Lipan, and the Kiowa-___ peoples.

Arizona Territory
1. ___ comprised the present-day state of Arizona and part of southern Nevada. It existed between 1863 and 1912.
2. In February 1863, during the American Civil War, Congress established ___ by splitting off the western portion of the New Mexico Territory.

Basin and Ridge
1. The ___ Region is south of the Transition Zone; it occupies a small strip of land along the western border with California.
2. Mountain ranges of the ___ Region include Chiricahua, Gila, Huachuca, Hualapai, Pinaleno, Santa Catalina, Santa Rita, and Superstition. These ranges are separated by low, fertile valleys.

Bolo Tie(s)
1. The ___ is the official neckwear for Arizona. 2. Most ___ are made of leather cord and have a silver or turquoise buckle.

Border
1. These states ___ Arizona: Utah, New Mexico, Nevada and California.
2. Arizona has an international ___: Mexico.

Buttes
1. Mesas and ___ are two types of flat-topped hills with steep sides.
2. Mesas and ___ are similar, but ___ are smaller. Both are smaller and more isolated than a plateau.

Cactus Wren
1. The ___ is the state bird. It is native to the deserts of the Southwest.
2. Found in arid regions, the ___ nests in cactus plants. It gets almost all of its water from its food.

César E. Chávez
1. This labor-rights leader and civil-rights activist was born in Yuma.
2. The slogan of this civil-rights leader was, *"Sí, se puede,"* or "Yes, it can be done." It became the motto of the United Farm Workers.

Climate (-ic)
1. Arizona has three basic ___ conditions based on average annual precipitation and mean temperature: desert, steppe and highland.
2. Arizona's weather is often categorized as hot and dry, but the state's ___ is actually quite varied.

Arizona Bingo

Cochise
1. ___ was a chief of the Chokonen band of the Chiricahua Apache. A county in Arizona is named for him.
2. This Chiricahua Apache was the leader of an uprising that began in 1861. In 1872 a treaty was finally negotiated with the help of Tom Jeffords, ___'s only white friend.

Colorado Plateau
1. The ___ covers the northern 2/5 of the state.
2. This major land area is characterized by mostly flat, level land. The Colorado River runs through the region, carving the Grand Canyon.

Copper
1. ___ is the most important mined product. Arizona produces more ___ than any other state.
2. Large amounts of gold, molybdenum, and silver are recovered as by-products of mining ___ ore.

Counties
1. There are 15 ___ in the state of Arizona.
2. Phoenix is in Maricopa ___, the most populous.

Crop(s)
1. Lettuce comprises about 20% of the state's total ___ production.
2. In addition to lettuce, important ___ include cotton, hay, cantaloupes, barley, potatoes, and wheat.

Francisco Vasquez de Coronado
1. This Spanish conquistador visited parts of what are now the southwestern United States between 1540 and 1542.
2. ___ had hoped to conquer the mythical Seven Cities of Gold.

Executive Branch
1. The ___ of state government includes the governor, the secretary of state, the attorney general, the treasurer, and the superintendent of public instruction.
2. The head of the ___ is the governor. The present-day governor is [fill in].

Flag
1. The lower half of the state ___ is a field of blue. The top half represents the 13 original colonies and the western setting sun.
2. The copper star in the center of the state ___ identifies Arizona as the largest producer of copper in the United States.

Flagstaff
1. Lowell Observatory is in ___.
2. This city in northern Arizona is named after a flagpole made of Ponderosa pine.

Gadsden Purchase
1. The ___ was an 1853 agreement to buy a strip of land in what is now the southern U.S. so that a railroad to the Gulf of California could be built.
2. The ___ included present-day southern Arizona and southwestern New Mexico; it is named after the U.S. minister to Mexico, who was responsible for the deal.

Arizona Bingo

Geronimo 1. Cochise, Mangas Coloradas, and ___ were three Apache leaders who fought against expansion into Apache tribal lands. 2. Exaggerated reports made ___ the most feared and infamous Apache. He surrendered to the U.S. authorities is 1886. While still a prisoner of war, in his old age he became a celebrity and appeared in fairs.	**Grand Canyon** 1. The ___ is considered one of the natural wonders of the world. Arizona is known as the ___ State. 2. The ___ was carved by the Colorado River. It is 277 river miles long, up to 18 miles wide, and a mile deep.
Hoover Dam 1. ___ is a concrete dam in the Black Canyon of the Colorado River; it is on the border between Arizona and Nevada. 2. It was once called Boulder Dam.	**Hopi** 1. The traditional homes of the ___ are multi-story complexes made of adobe called pueblos. 2. During special ceremonies ___ men dress in costumes and masks to represent katsina spirits.
Humphreys Peak 1. At 12,633 feet, ___ is the highest point in the state. 2. ___ is located within the Kachina Peaks Wilderness in the Coconino National Forest, about 11 miles north of Flagstaff.	**Judicial Branch** 1. The ___ interprets what our laws mean and makes decisions about the laws and those who break them. 2. It is made up of several court systems, the highest of which is the state Supreme Court.
Lake Havasu 1. ___ was created by by Parker Dam. The London Bridge is one of its main attractions. 2. ___ City on the eastern shore of ___ is part of the Sonoran Desert.	**Lake Mead** 1. ___ is America's largest man-made reservoir. 2. ___ was created by the damming of the Colorado River.
Legislative Branch 1. The ___ comprises the Arizona Senate and the Arizona House of Representatives. 2. The ___ makes the laws.	**Livestock** 1. The most important ___ product is cattle, including calves. 2. Beef cattle, including calves, is the leading source of farm income. Hogs, sheep and lambs are other ___ products.

Arizona Bingo

© Barbara M. Peller

Manufacture 1. The ___ of computer and electronic equipment and electronic components are important industries. 2. The ___ of transportation equipment and chemicals are also important industries.	**Monument Valley** 1. ___ is a region of the Colorado Plateau. This region is characterized by sandstone Buttes that reach heights of 400 to 1,000 feet. 2. ___ Navajo Tribal Park is a popular tourist destination. The vivid red color comes from iron oxide exposed in the weathered siltstone.
Motto 1. The state ___, *"Ditat Deus,"* is on the state seal. 2. Translated from the Latin, the state ___ is "God enriches."	**Navajo** 1. It is believed that the ___ began working with turquoise after returning from the "Long Walk" to and from Fort Sumner, New Mexico, in 1868. 2. A traditional eight-sided, one-room ___ home is called a hogan.
Palo Verde 1. The ___ is the state tree. 2. The name of this state tree is Spanish for "green stick."	**Petrified Wood** 1. ___ is the state fossil. 2. ___ is the name given to the fossilized remains of trees or tree-like plants.
Phoenix 1. ___ is the capital and largest city in Arizona. It is the county seat of Maricopa County. 2. At over 16,000 acres, South Mountain Park in ___ is the largest city park in the world.	**Pueblos** 1. Twenty-one ___ still exist today. Taos, Acoma, Zuni, and Hopi are the best known. 2. Wupatki National Monument was established by President Coolidge in 1924 to preserve Citadel and Wupatki ___.
Ridge-nosed Rattlesnake 1. The Arizona ___ is the state reptile. 2. This reptile is characterized by its white facial stripes and the distinctive ridge along each side of its nose,	**Ringtail** 1. The ___ is the state mammal. 2. The ___ is sometimes called a miner's cat, but it is actually a relative of the raccoon and coatimundi.
Arizona Bingo	© Barbara M. Peller

River(s) 1. The Gila, the Colorado, the Little Colorado, and the Bill Williams are ___ in Arizona. 2. Arizona, California, Colorado, Nevada, New Mexico and Utah all depend on the Colorado ___ and its tributaries for water.	**Saguaro Cactus** 1. This plant is on the state quarter. 2. The ___ blossom is the state flower.
Seal 1. Under the motto in the Great ___ is a scene that portrays Arizona's landscape, climate, and industry. 2. The scene on the Great ___ of Arizona includes a miner, a sun, and a fertile field.	**Sedona** 1. The picturesque city of ___ is surrounded by red-rock monoliths named Coffeepot, Cathedral and Thunder Mountain. 2. At the north end of ___ is the beautiful Oak Creek Canyon.
Tohono O'odham 1. The conquistadors called them Papago, but these Native Americans are now known as ___, or "Desert People." 2. The lands of the ___ Nation are located within the Sonoran Desert. Their largest community, Sells, functions as its capital.	**Transition Zone** 1. The ___ is south of the Colorado Plateau and north of the Arizona Basin and Ridge Region. 2. The ___ is characterized by rugged mountain ranges and valleys. The Mazatzal, Santa Maria, Sierra Ancha, and White mountain ranges are in the ___; so is the Salt River Canyon.
Tree Frog 1. The Arizona ___ is the state amphibian. 2. This tiny amphibian is only about 3/4 of an inch to 2 inches long.	**Turquoise** 1. ___ is the state gemstone. 2. Most important deposits of ___ are located near or in copper deposits; therefore, it is not surprising that much of the world's finest-quality ___ comes from Arizona.
Tucson 1. San Xavier del Bac Mission in ___ is the oldest intact European structure in Arizona. A National Historic Landmark, it was founded by Father Eusebio Kino in 1692. 2. The main campus of the University of Arizona is located in ___.	**Union** 1. Arizona entered the ___ on February 14, 1912. 2. Arizona was the 48th state to enter the ___.

Arizona Bingo

Pueblos	Anthem	Arizona Territory	Flagstaff	Bolo Tie(s)
Executive Branch	Apache(s)	Turquoise	Livestock	River(s)
Tree Frog	Legislative Branch		Palo Verde	Tucson
Transition Zone	Ringtail	Tohono O'odham	Lake Mead	Monument Valley
Navajo	Grand Canyon	Counties	Seal	Humphreys Peak

Arizona Bingo

Transition Zone	Tree Frog	Hopi	Ridge-nosed Rattlesnake	Lake Havasu
Monument Valley	Crop(s)	Cactus Wren	Ringtail	Motto
Climate (-ic)	Grand Canyon		Hoover Dam	Tohono O'odham
Petrified Wood	Phoenix	Legislative Branch	Union	Bolo Tie(s)
River(s)	Turquoise	Counties	Executive Branch	Seal

© Barbara M. Peller

Arizona Bingo

Grand Canyon	Tohono O'odham	Crop(s)	Lake Mead	Tree Frog
Monument Valley	Apache(s)	César E. Chávez	Anthem	Geronimo
Ringtail	Turquoise		Motto	Basin and Ridge
Legislative Branch	Climate (-ic)	Navajo	Petrified Wood	Hopi
Seal	Cochise	Counties	Union	Lake Havasu

Arizona
Bingo

Arizona Bingo

Legislative Branch	Motto	Arizona Territory	Cochise	Lake Havasu
Manufacture	Buttes	Anthem	Ridge-nosed Rattlesnake	Tree Frog
Palo Verde	Petrified Wood		Humphreys Peak	Flagstaff
Tohono O'odham	Apache(s)	Turquoise	Counties	Cactus Wren
Colorado Plateau	River(s)	Border	Seal	Tucson

Arizona Bingo

River(s)	Bolo Tie(s)	Ringtail	Cactus Wren	Cochise
Manufacture	Tohono O'odham	César E. Chávez	Hoover Dam	Apache(s)
Arizona Territory	Tucson		Livestock	Gadsden Purchase
Humphreys Peak	Lake Havasu	Pueblos	Union	Copper
Crop(s)	Counties	Tree Frog	Legislative Branch	Palo Verde

Arizona Bingo: Card No. 5

Arizona Bingo

Basin and Ridge	Motto	Hopi	Lake Havasu	Tucson
Lake Mead	Ringtail	Copper	Anthem	Tree Frog
Ridge-nosed Rattlesnake	Colorado Plateau		Buttes	Hoover Dam
Counties	Navajo	Union	Border	Arizona Territory
Monument Valley	Cactus Wren	Pueblos	Palo Verde	Francisco Vasquez de Coronado

Arizona Bingo

Pueblos	Motto	Gadsden Purchase	Tohono O'odham	Crop(s)
Monument Valley	Lake Havasu	Grand Canyon	Apache(s)	Manufacture
Tucson	Flagstaff		Hoover Dam	Buttes
Legislative Branch	Petrified Wood	César E. Chávez	Transition Zone	Climate (-ic)
Counties	Cochise	Union	Border	Basin and Ridge

Arizona Bingo

Palo Verde	Motto	Flag	Lake Mead	Buttes
Manufacture	Arizona Territory	Ridge-nosed Rattlesnake	Tucson	Cactus Wren
Francisco Vasquez de Coronado	Cochise		Lake Havasu	Bolo Tie(s)
Seal	Legislative Branch	Transition Zone	Colorado Plateau	Petrified Wood
Turquoise	Counties	Border	Ringtail	Monument Valley

Arizona Bingo: Card No. 8

Arizona Bingo

Hoover Dam	Crop(s)	Grand Canyon	Francisco Vasquez de Coronado	Cochise
Colorado Plateau	Lake Havasu	Palo Verde	Ringtail	Motto
Geronimo	Pueblos		Apache(s)	Flag
Copper	Bolo Tie(s)	Navajo	Livestock	Gadsden Purchase
Petrified Wood	Union	César E. Chávez	Transition Zone	Humphreys Peak

Arizona Bingo

Transition Zone	Lake Mead	Buttes	Ridge-nosed Rattlesnake	Francisco Vasquez de Coronado
Tucson	Cactus Wren	Anthem	Apache(s)	Lake Havasu
Cochise	Motto		Flagstaff	Climate (-ic)
Navajo	Humphreys Peak	Copper	Union	Geronimo
César E. Chávez	Monument Valley	Hopi	River(s)	Palo Verde

Arizona Bingo: Card No. 10

Arizona Bingo

Basin and Ridge	Motto	Ringtail	Copper	Monument Valley
Flag	Geronimo	Livestock	Hoover Dam	Anthem
Manufacture	Lake Havasu		Hopi	Grand Canyon
César E. Chávez	Tree Frog	Union	Cochise	Transition Zone
Colorado Plateau	Counties	Pueblos	Border	Crop(s)

Arizona Bingo: Card No. 11

Arizona Bingo

Crop(s)	Bolo Tie(s)	Geronimo	Lake Mead	Hoover Dam
Grand Canyon	Monument Valley	Arizona Territory	Border	Apache(s)
Pueblos	Gadsden Purchase		Tucson	Ridge-nosed Rattlesnake
Counties	Petrified Wood	Lake Havasu	Transition Zone	Manufacture
Motto	Flag	Cochise	Colorado Plateau	Cactus Wren

Arizona Bingo

Copper	Bolo Tie(s)	Basin and Ridge	Geronimo	Tucson
Arizona Territory	Flag	Lake Havasu	Hoover Dam	Climate (-ic)
Lake Mead	Cactus Wren		Grand Canyon	Gadsden Purchase
Palo Verde	Union	Buttes	Cochise	Transition Zone
Counties	Humphreys Peak	Border	Pueblos	Livestock

Arizona Bingo: Card No. 13

© Barbara M. Peller

Arizona Bingo

Arizona Bingo

Executive Branch	Lake Havasu	Ringtail	Hoover Dam	Colorado Plateau
Cactus Wren	Pueblos	Geronimo	Apache(s)	Motto
Copper	Flagstaff		Hopi	César E. Chávez
Humphreys Peak	Union	Cochise	Buttes	Basin and Ridge
Counties	Ridge-nosed Rattlesnake	Climate (-ic)	Monument Valley	Palo Verde

Arizona Bingo: Card No. 14

Arizona Bingo

Livestock	Hoover Dam	Ringtail	Crop(s)	Lake Mead
Basin and Ridge	Hopi	Anthem	Arizona Territory	Colorado Plateau
Tucson	Pueblos		Tree Frog	Motto
Counties	Geronimo	Flag	Union	Copper
Monument Valley	Petrified Wood	Border	Francisco Vasquez de Coronado	Grand Canyon

Arizona Bingo: Card No. 15

Arizona Bingo

Buttes	Geronimo	Flag	Francisco Vasquez de Coronado	Phoenix
Ridge-nosed Rattlesnake	Climate (-ic)	Gadsden Purchase	Manufacture	Flagstaff
Copper	Bolo Tie(s)		Tucson	Grand Canyon
Legislative Branch	Cactus Wren	Counties	Livestock	Transition Zone
Colorado Plateau	Sedona	Border	Petrified Wood	Motto

Arizona Bingo

César E. Chávez	Saguaro Cactus	Judicial Branch	Geronimo	Executive Branch
Livestock	Colorado Plateau	Union	Flagstaff	Gadsden Purchase
Hoover Dam	Palo Verde		Sedona	Flag
Humphreys Peak	Monument Valley	Transition Zone	Ringtail	Climate (-ic)
Navajo	Copper	Crop(s)X	Lake Mead	Bolo Tie(s)

Arizona Bingo: Card No. 17

Arizona Bingo

Francisco Vasquez de Coronado	Cochise	Cactus Wren	Copper	Ridge-nosed Rattlesnake
Motto	César E. Chávez	Navajo	Tucson	Colorado Plateau
Hoover Dam	Climate (-ic)		Judicial Branch	Arizona Territory
Bolo Tie(s)	Anthem	Union	Transition Zone	Hopi
Sedona	Geronimo	Ringtail	Saguaro Cactus	Basin and Ridge

Arizona Bingo: Card No. 18

Arizona Bingo

Tucson	Basin and Ridge	Geronimo	Flag	Transition Zone
Livestock	Lake Mead	Motto	Crop(s)	Flagstaff
Saguaro Cactus	Cochise		Apache(s)	Tree Frog
Hopi	Sedona	Navajo	Petrified Wood	Judicial Branch
Arizona Territory	Phoenix	Monument Valley	Palo Verde	Border

Arizona Bingo: Card No. 19

Arizona Bingo

Executive Branch	Saguaro Cactus	Lake Mead	Geronimo	Border
Cactus Wren	Grand Canyon	Manufacture	Navajo	Ridge-nosed Rattlesnake
Bolo Tie(s)	Gadsden Purchase		Legislative Branch	Anthem
River(s)	Turquoise	Seal	Petrified Wood	Sedona
Tohono O'odham	Palo Verde	Phoenix	Transition Zone	Judicial Branch

Arizona Bingo: Card No. 20

Arizona Bingo

Livestock	Basin and Ridge	Manufacture	Geronimo	River(s)
Bolo Tie(s)	Judicial Branch	Buttes	Flag	Pueblos
Climate (-ic)	Monument Valley		Saguaro Cactus	Ringtail
Navajo	Crop(s)	Sedona	Humphreys Peak	Palo Verde
Legislative Branch	Phoenix	Border	César E. Chávez	Petrified Wood

Arizona Bingo

Francisco Vasquez de Coronado	Hopi	Judicial Branch	Arizona Territory	Copper
Ridge-nosed Rattlesnake	Lake Mead	Tree Frog	Flag	Apache(s)
Cactus Wren	Flagstaff		Pueblos	Gadsden Purchase
Sedona	Humphreys Peak	Petrified Wood	Anthem	Manufacture
Phoenix	César E. Chávez	Saguaro Cactus	Climate (-ic)	Anthem

Arizona Bingo

Buttes	Saguaro Cactus	Crop(s)	Arizona Territory	Border
Basin and Ridge	Executive Branch	Monument Valley	Livestock	Anthem
Hopi	Copper		Seal	Pueblos
Climate (-ic)	Phoenix	Sedona	César E. Chávez	Petrified Wood
River(s)	Turquoise	Palo Verde	Navajo	Judicial Branch

Arizona Bingo

Buttes	Palo Verde	Executive Branch	Saguaro Cactus	Flag
Judicial Branch	Border	Manufacture	Ridge-nosed Rattlesnake	Pueblos
Gadsden Purchase	Francisco Vasquez de Coronado		Copper	Climate (-ic)
River(s)	Seal	Sedona	César E. Chávez	Bolo Tie(s)
Tohono O'odham	Legislative Branch	Phoenix	Lake Mead	Turquoise

Arizona Bingo: Card No. 24

Arizona Bingo

Legislative Branch	Manufacture	Saguaro Cactus	Ringtail	Judicial Branch
Anthem	Bolo Tie(s)	Livestock	Buttes	Apache(s)
Humphreys Peak	Flag		Seal	Sedona
Tree Frog	River(s)	Turquoise	Phoenix	Flagstaff
Border	Executive Branch	Cactus Wren	Colorado Plateau	Tohono O'odham

Arizona Bingo

Judicial Branch	Saguaro Cactus	Hopi	Ridge-nosed Rattlesnake	Francisco Vasquez de Coronado
Navajo	Lake Mead	Flag	Executive Branch	Buttes
Humphreys Peak	Seal		Flagstaff	Legislative Branch
César E. Chávez	Arizona Territory	River(s)	Phoenix	Sedona
Gadsden Purchase	Colorado Plateau	Ringtail	Turquoise	Tohono O'odham

Arizona Bingo

Hopi	Cactus Wren	Saguaro Cactus	Executive Branch	Grand Canyon
River(s)	Seal	Livestock	Sedona	Apache(s)
Union	Turquoise		Phoenix	Legislative Branch
Francisco Vasquez de Coronado	Basin and Ridge	Manufacture	Tohono O'odham	Anthem
Colorado Plateau	Flagstaff	Judicial Branch	Tree Frog	Gadsden Purchase

Arizona Bingo

Hopi	Executive Branch	Tree Frog	Saguaro Cactus	Buttes
Grand Canyon	Judicial Branch	Seal	Ridge-nosed Rattlesnake	Flagstaff
Turquoise	Climate (-ic)		Gadsden Purchase	Navajo
Transition Zone	Francisco Vasquez de Coronado	Monument Valley	Phoenix	Sedona
Arizona Territory	Hoover Dam	Colorado Plateau	Tohono O'odham	River(s)

Arizona Bingo

Judicial Branch	Executive Branch	Francisco Vasquez de Coronado	Livestock	Hoover Dam
Petrified Wood	Navajo	Manufacture	Gadsden Purchase	Tree Frog
Humphreys Peak	Seal		Apache(s)	Saguaro Cactus
Grand Canyon	River(s)	Lake Havasu	Phoenix	Sedona
Buttes	Flag	Tohono O'odham	Basin and Ridge	Turquoise

Arizona Bingo: Card No. 29

Arizona Bingo

Cochise	Saguaro Cactus	Ridge-nosed Rattlesnake	Hoover Dam	Sedona
Anthem	Executive Branch	Hopi	Flagstaff	Apache(s)
Humphreys Peak	Copper		Gadsden Purchase	Manufacture
Tohono O'odham	Basin and Ridge	Arizona Territory	Phoenix	Seal
River(s)	Tucson	Turquoise	Judicial Branch	Tree Frog

www.ingramcontent.com/pod-product-compliance
Lightning Source LLC
LaVergne TN
LVHW061337060426
835511LV00014B/1962